cocktails

the perfect guide to cocktail making **STEP-BY-STEP**

cocktails

the perfect guide to cocktail making

STEP-BY-STEP

This edition published by Parragon Books Ltd in 2013
LOVE FOOD is an imprint of Parragon Books Ltd

Parragon Books Ltd
Chartist House
15-17 Trim Street
Bath, BA1 1HA, UK
www.parragon.com/lovefood

ISBN: 978-1-4454-8281-1

Printed in China

Cover design by Geoff Borin
Internal design by Talking Design
Introduction by Paul Martin
Edited by Fiona Biggs

Notes for the Reader
All spoon measurements are level: teaspoons are assumed to be 5 ml, and tablespoons are
assumed to be 15 ml and one measure is assumed to be 25 ml/ ¾ fl oz. Unless otherwise
stated, milk is assumed to be full fat and eggs are medium-sized. Recipes using raw eggs
should be avoided by infants, the elderly, pregnant women, convalescents and anyone suffering
from an illness. Please consume alcohol responsibly.

contents

introduction

This beautiful book with its delightful recipes and moreish photography will quickly become an indispensable tool for any budding mixologist.
In this comprehensive collection you'll find punches for parties, short drinks for unwinding of an evening and impressive crowd-pleasers for entertaining.
All recipes are simply written to make them easy to follow and will guarantee even the novice cocktail-maker a winning result every time.

Cocktails have played a colourful part in modern history and cemented their place in popular culture. The history of the first cocktails remains a mystery – which has led to a number of popular folk tales. One of the more popular stories that's been told recounts how, during the revolutionary war, American and French soldiers frequented Betsy's tavern to enjoy a famous alcoholic concoction of her own design, known as 'Betsy's Bracer'. One night, amidst wild drinking and parties, one of the American soldiers stole a couple of roosters from a neighbour's garden. He toasted his theft with his drinking companions, saying "Here's to the divine liquor which is as delicious to the palate as the cock's tail is beautiful to the eye", to which a French officer is said to have responded "Vive le Cocktail!" – and with that, the term cocktail was apparently born!

Since their conception cocktails have seen trends come and go – from the days of the practical cocktail (mixers were used to disguise the flavours of homemade spirits during American prohibition years), to the fancy, frivolous cocktails favoured over the eighties and the pared-back, stylish cocktails made famous by stage and screen characters in the noughties.

Why you need this book
The art of the skilled mixologist is underpinned by a set of easy-to-follow principles that can set almost anyone on the right track to producing an extensive range of cocktails and mixed drinks. In this book, all the necessary skills are laid bare, allowing the reader to effortlessly apply them to the broad range of featured cocktail recipes. Simply read up on the terminology and techniques that follow and get started on the recipes – before long you'll be mixing and shaking with the best of them.

mixing methods

Creating a cocktail is not brain surgery but it does require the deft touch of a skilled mixologist. The better your mixing techniques, the finer the quality of the resulting drink. In fact, mixing a cocktail is not simply a matter of throwing the ingredients together in a glass, giving them a stir and hoping for the best – there are numerous mixing methods, all of which have benefits behind their recommended usage.

The following are the most commonly used methods and the ones to be found within these pages.

> **Shaking:** This is when we add all the ingredients, with a scoop of ice, to the shaker and then shake vigorously for approximately 5 seconds. The benefit of shaking is that the drink is rapidly mixed, chilled and aerated – you will notice that after the drink has been shaken, the outside of the shaker itself will be lightly frosted. Shaking a cocktail will also dilute the drink quite significantly.

>1 >2 >3

>1 >2 >3

This dilution is a necessary part of the process and gives shaken recipes the requisite balance of taste, strength and temperature.

In addition, we may also choose to shake a drink that includes an ingredient that would not combine effectively with a less vigorous form of mixing, such as egg white.

> **Stirring:** With this technique we once again add all the ingredients to a scoop of ice, but this time combine them in a mixing glass or small jug. We then stir the ingredients together using a long-handled bar spoon.

As with the shaken method this allows us to blend and chill the ingredients, but unlike the shaken method the erosion of the ice is significantly less and consequently we are able to control the level of dilution and keep it to a minimum. This simple but vital technique is essential for a number of drinks that do not require much dilution, like a classic Dry Martini.

> **Building:** To 'build' a drink, we quite simply make it in the glass, as you would with a gin and tonic. It is important to follow the instructions for built cocktails as the order of ingredients can change from drink to drink and this can impact upon the finished flavours.

> **Muddling:** We muddle ingredients when we are trying to extract juice or oils from the pulp or skin of a fruit, herb or spice. A muddler is simply a pestle that we would use to crush the ingredient accordingly – you can get a specific tool for the job, or alternatively use a wooden rolling pin.

> **Blending:** As the name suggests, this is when the ingredients are combined in a blender! The goal for most blended drinks is that they are served with a smooth consistency. Accordingly, the ingredients are usually blended with a scoop of crushed ice

and often include items like fresh fruit, that can't be shaken or stirred.

> **Layering:** When creating layers in a cocktail it's important to follow the instructions, as the heavier spirits or liqueurs must go into the glass first.

The first, base layer should be poured into the centre of the glass, without getting any down the sides, if possible. To create the second layer, we turn a teaspoon upside down, with the tip touching the inside of the glass, and pour the liquid slowly over the back of the spoon (moving it up the glass as the level within the glass rises). This is then repeated, with any remaining liquid ingredients, using a clean teaspoon with each new layer.

the right ice

The topic of ice is a broad one within the world of mixology. Get the ice right and you have the foundations of a great cocktail, get it wrong and it can demote a great drink to just average.

The job of ice is two-fold – during the mixing process it helps to chill and actively mixes the ingredients, and once the drink is served it works to keep the cocktail cold and keeps further dilution to a minimum. There are three types of ice used in the cocktail recipes that follow, each has distinctive properties which complement the styles and flavours within a drink.

> **Cubed ice:** This is generally used to finish a drink. It's important to remember that the more ice you have in your glass, the colder it will keep the drink, the slower the ice will melt and so the less your finished cocktail will be diluted. Ice cubes can be made in your freezer at home with a simple ice tray – 2-cm/¾-inch cubes are the best size for finishing most drinks. These cubes can be broken down and used to make cracked and crushed ice as necessary.

> **Cracked ice:** This is smaller than full ice cubes and is generally used in a shaker to chill the liquid ingredients before straining. To create cracked ice from whole ice cubes, simply wrap in a clean, dry tea towel and give them a gentle knock with a rolling pin or other implement. You should aim to break or crack the ice into pieces no smaller than a halved cube.

> **Crushed ice:** This is perfect for blended drinks as it speeds up the mixing process and rapidly freezes the whole concoction. In some drinks it is preferable to use cubed or cracked ice, as it allows us to pack the glass with the maximum amount of ice (cubes leave greater gaps). To create crushed ice from whole ice cubes, wrap in a tea towel and break with repeated, moderate knocks with a rolling pin or other implement. You should aim to break the ice cubes into very small pieces, of a consistent size.

>1 >2 >3

pick your glassware

The selection of the right glassware is an often underestimated part of the cocktail-making process. For some mixologists the glass is actually considered to be as important as the ingredients themselves – the shape, style and size all impact on the visual perception and overall enjoyment of the drink. As a consequence we have all come to associate drinks with specific glassware – consider the Cosmopolitan, which is now synonymous with a stylish yet simple Martini glass, or Long Island Iced Tea, which surely could be served in nothing but a tall, ice-filled glass.

Conversely, serving a cocktail in the wrong glass, or one generally associated with a different drink, will detract from the presentation and experience. For this reason, each one of the glasses recommended in this book have been chosen to enhance the cocktail that they have been assigned to.

final flourishes

Many consider the garnish to be the defining element of a cocktail. In some cases, the garnish can be synonymous with the drink itself – think of the Piña Colada with its obligatory pineapple slice. As a result they are often a vital ingredient but in most other cases a garnish appears primarily for aesthetics.

There are a number of basic guidelines that are used for adding the final flourishes to a drink, but ultimately the way in which we may choose to garnish a cocktail is often up to the imagination and artistic flair of the mixologist. One of the simplest rules to follow is to match the garnish to the featured flavours. Think of your cocktail as a blank canvas – in this book we have recommended some simple garnishes to go with the recipes, but if you want to have a bit of fun, throw the rule book in the bin and just have a go at creating your own.

Remember – enjoy your drinks, don't make yourself ill and be aware of the government's current guidelines on alcohol consumption. Experiment with this book and, to get the maximum pleasure out of your cocktails, follow the recipes, perfect and use well honed mixing methods, choose the right glass, garnish with care and above all, enjoy!

Paul Martin is a multi award-winning cocktail mixologist, author of numerous cocktail books and twice Guinness World Record holder (having mixed 196 different cocktails, one at a time, in 60 minutes). Over the last 10 years he has earned a reputation as one of the most inspirational mentors in the drinks industry, running mixology courses for countless UK high street brands. Paul has also appeared on numerous UK television programmes in his capacity as a cocktail expert.

>4>5>6

classic cocktails

martini

serves 1

ingredients
4–6 cracked ice
  cubes
3 measures gin
1 tsp dry vermouth,
  or to taste
cocktail olive,
  to decorate

>1 Put the cracked ice cubes into a cocktail shaker.

>2 Pour the gin and vermouth over the ice cubes.

>3 Shake until well frosted. Strain into a chilled cocktail glass.

>4 Decorate with the olive.

Serve immediately.

margarita

serves 1

ingredients
2 lime wedges
coarse salt
4–6 cracked ice
  cubes
3 measures white
  tequila
1 measure Triple Sec
  or Cointreau
2 measures lime
  juice

>1 Rub the rim of a chilled cocktail glass with a lime wedge.

>2 Dip in a saucer of coarse salt.

>3 Put the cracked ice cubes into a cocktail shaker. Pour over the tequila, Triple Sec and lime juice and shake vigorously until well frosted. Strain into the glass.

Serve immediately.

>4 Decorate with the remaining lime wedge.

club mojito

serves 1

ingredients
1 tsp sugar syrup
6 fresh mint leaves,
  plus extra to
  decorate
juice of ½ lime
4–6 cracked ice
  cubes
2 measures
  Jamaican rum
soda water
dash Angostura
  bitters

>1 Put the sugar syrup, mint leaves and lime juice into a lowball glass.

>2 Muddle the mint leaves, then add the cracked ice cubes and the rum.

>3 Top up with soda water.

>4 Finish with the Angostura bitters and decorate with the remaining mint leaves.

Serve immediately.

bellini

serves 1

ingredients
1 lemon wedge
caster sugar
1 measure peach
 juice
3 measures
 champagne,
 chilled

>1 Rub the rim of a chilled champagne flute with the lemon wedge.

>2 Put the sugar in a saucer, then dip the rim of the flute in it.

>**3** Pour the peach juice into the flute.

Serve immediately.

>**4** Top up with the champagne.

23

bloody mary

serves 1

ingredients
4–6 cracked ice
  cubes
dash hot pepper
  sauce
dash Worcestershire
  sauce
2 measures vodka
6 measures tomato
  juice
juice of ½ lemon
pinch celery salt
pinch cayenne
  pepper
celery stick and
  lemon slice,
  to decorate

>1 Put the cracked ice cubes into a cocktail shaker. Dash the hot pepper sauce and Worcestershire sauce over the ice.

>2 Add the vodka and tomato juice.

Serve immediately.

>**3** Add the lemon juice and shake vigorously until well frosted.

>**4** Strain into a tall, chilled glass, add the celery salt and cayenne pepper and decorate with the celery stick and lemon slice.

25

manhattan

serves 1

ingredients
4–6 cracked ice
 cubes
dash Angostura
 bitters
3 measures rye
 whiskey
1 measure sweet
 vermouth
cocktail cherry,
 to decorate

>1 Put the cracked ice cubes
into a cocktail shaker.

>2 Pour the liquid ingredients over the
ice cubes.

>3 Shake vigorously until well frosted.

Serve immediately.

>4 Strain into a chilled cocktail glass and decorate with the cherry.

cosmopolitan

serves 1

ingredients

4–6 cracked ice
  cubes
2 measures vodka
1 measure Triple Sec
1 measure lime
  juice
1 measure
  cranberry juice
orange peel strip,
  to decorate

>1 Put the cracked ice cubes
into a cocktail shaker.

>2 Pour the liquid ingredients over the
ice cubes.

Serve immediately.

>3 Shake vigorously until well frosted.

>4 Strain into a chilled cocktail glass and decorate with the orange peel.

long island iced tea

serves 1

ingredients
cracked ice
2 measures vodka
1 measure gin
1 measure white
 tequila
1 measure white
 rum
½ measure white
 crème de menthe
2 measures lemon
 juice
1 tsp caster sugar
cola
lime wedge,
 to decorate

>1 Put 4–6 cracked ice cubes into a cocktail shaker. Pour all the liquid ingredients except the cola over the ice, add the sugar and shake vigorously until well frosted.

>2 Half-fill a tall glass with cracked ice and strain over the cocktail.

>**3** Top up with cola.

Serve immediately.

>**4** Decorate with the lime wedge.

sidecar

serves 1

ingredients
4–6 cracked ice
 cubes
2 measures brandy
1 measure Triple Sec
1 measure lemon
 juice
1 orange

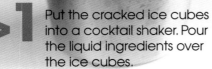 Put the cracked ice cubes into a cocktail shaker. Pour the liquid ingredients over the ice cubes.

 Shake vigorously until well frosted.

>3 Peel a strip of orange zest, to decorate.

Serve immediately.

>4 Strain into a chilled cocktail glass and decorate with the orange peel.

singapore sling
serves 1

ingredients
cracked ice
2 measures gin
1 measure cherry
  brandy
1 measure lemon
  juice
1 tsp grenadine
soda water
lime peel strips and
  cocktail cherries,
  to decorate

>1 Put 4–6 cracked ice cubes into a cocktail shaker and pour over the gin.

>2 Pour over the cherry brandy, lemon juice and grenadine and shake vigorously until well frosted.

>3 Half-fill a chilled glass with cracked ice cubes and strain over the cocktail.

>4 Top up with soda water and decorate with the lime peel and cherries.

Serve immediately.

old-fashioned

serves 1

ingredients
1 sugar cube
dash of Angostura
  bitters
1 tsp water
2 measures
  bourbon or rye
  whiskey
4–6 cracked ice
  cubes
lemon peel twist,
  to decorate

>**1** Place the sugar cube in a small, chilled lowball glass.

>**2** Add the Angostura bitters and water. Stir until the sugar has dissolved.

>3 Pour in the bourbon and stir.

>4 Add the cracked ice cubes and decorate with the lemon peel.

Serve immediately.

daiquiri

serves 1

ingredients

4–6 cracked ice
  cubes
½ tsp caster sugar,
  dissolved in 1 tbsp
  boiling water
¼ measure lime
  juice
½ tsp sugar syrup
lime wedge,
  to decorate

>1 Put the cracked ice cubes
into a cocktail shaker.

>2 Pour the rum, lime juice and sugar
water over the ice cubes.

>3 Shake vigorously until well frosted.

Serve immediately.

>4 Strain into a chilled cocktail glass and decorate with a wedge of lime.

39

moscow mule

serves 1

ingredients
cracked ice
2 measures vodka
1 measure lime
  juice
ginger beer
lime wedge,
  to decorate

>1 Put 4–6 cracked ice cubes into a cocktail shaker.

>2 Pour the vodka and lime juice over the ice cubes and shake vigorously until well frosted.

>**3** Half-fill a chilled glass with cracked ice and strain over the cocktail.

>**4** Top up with ginger beer and decorate with the lime wedge.

Serve immediately.

hurricane

serves 1

ingredients

4–6 cracked ice
   cubes
4 measures dark
   rum
1 measure lemon
   juice
2 measures orange
   and passion
   fruit juice
soda water
orange slices and
   cocktail cherries,
   to decorate

>1 Put the cracked ice cubes into a cocktail shaker.

>2 Add the rum, lemon juice and orange and passion fruit juice and shake until well combined.

Serve immediately.

>3 Pour the cocktail into a tall, chilled glass.

>4 Top up with soda water and decorate with the orange slices and cherries.

zombie

serves 1

ingredients
4–6 crushed ice
  cubes
2 measures dark rum
2 measures white
  rum
1 measure golden
  rum
1 measure Triple Sec
1 measure lime juice
1 measure orange
  juice
1 measure
  pineapple juice
1 measure guava
  juice
1 tbsp grenadine
1 tbsp orgeat syrup
1 tsp Pernod
fresh mint sprig and
  pineapple wedge,
  to decorate

>1 Put the crushed ice cubes into a cocktail shaker.

>2 Pour over the liquid ingredients and shake vigorously until well frosted.

>3 Pour the cocktail into a chilled glass.

>4 Decorate with the fresh mint and the pineapple wedge.

Serve immediately.

tom collins

serves 1

ingredients
4–6 cracked ice
  cubes
3 measures gin
2 measures lemon
  juice
½ measure sugar
  syrup
soda water
lemon slices,
  to decorate

>1 Put the cracked ice cubes into a cocktail shaker.

>2 Pour over the gin, lemon juice and sugar syrup and shake vigorously until well frosted.

>3 Strain into a chilled Collins glass.

>4 Top up with soda water and decorate with the lemon slices.

Serve immediately.

WOO-WOO

serves 1

ingredients
crushed ice
4 measures
  cranberry juice
2 measures vodka
2 measures peach
  schnapps

>1 Half-fill a chilled cocktail glass with crushed ice.

>2 Pour over the cranberry juice.

>**3** Add the vodka and peach schnapps.

>**4** Stir well to mix.

Serve immediately.

harvey wallbanger

serves 1

ingredients
cracked ice
3 measures vodka
8 measures orange
 juice
2 tsp Galliano
cocktail cherry and
 orange slice,
 to decorate

>1 Half-fill a tall glass with cracked ice cubes.

>2 Pour over the vodka and orange juice.

>3 Float the Galliano on top.

>4 Decorate with the cherry and the orange slice.

Serve immediately.

screwdriver

serves 1

ingredients
cracked ice
2 measures vodka
orange juice
orange slice,
 to decorate

>1 Fill a tall, chilled glass with cracked ice. Pour the vodka over the ice.

>2 Top up with orange juice.

>3 Stir well to mix.

>4 Decorate with the orange slice.

Serve immediately.

piña colada

serves 1

ingredients
4–6 crushed ice
  cubes
2 measures white
  rum
1 measure dark
  rum
3 measures
  pineapple juice
2 measures
  coconut cream
cocktail cherry and
  pineapple wedge,
  to decorate

>1 Put the crushed ice cubes in a blender. Pour over the white rum, dark rum and pineapple juice.

>2 Add the coconut cream to the blender and blend until smooth.

Serve immediately.

>3 Pour, without straining, into a chilled glass.

>4 Decorate with the cocktail cherry and the pineapple wedge.

caipirinha

serves 1

ingredients
6 lime wedges
2 tsp granulated
sugar
3 measures
cachaça
4–6 cracked
ice cubes

>1 Put the lime wedges in a chilled
lowball glass.

>2 Add the sugar.

>3 Muddle the lime wedges, then pour over the cachaça.

>4 Fill the glass with the cracked ice and stir well.

Serve immediately.

mai tai

serves 1

ingredients
4–6 cracked ice
  cubes
2 measures white rum
2 measures dark rum
1 measure orange
  curaçao
1 measure lime juice
1 tbsp orgeat syrup
1 tbsp grenadine

to decorate
pineapple wedge
pineapple leaves
cocktail cherry
orange peel twist

>1 Put the cracked ice cubes into a cocktail shaker. Pour over the white rum, dark rum, curaçao, lime juice, orgeat syrup and grenadine.

>2 Shake vigorously until well frosted and strain into a chilled glass.

>3 Dec   eapple wedge.

>4 Add the   cocktail cherry and oran

Serve immediately.

mimosa

serves 1

ingredients
cracked ice
1 passion fruit
½ measure orange
  curaçao
champagne,
  chilled
star fruit slice,
  to decorate

>1 Put the cracked ice cubes into a cocktail shaker.

>2 Scoop out the passion fruit flesh into the shaker.

Serve immediately.

>3 Add the curaçao and shake until frosted.

>4 Strain into a chilled champagne flute, top up with champagne and decorate with the star fruit slice.

tequila sunrise

serves 1

ingredients
4–6 cracked ice
  cubes
2 measures silver
  tequila
orange juice
1 measure grenadine
orange slice and
  cocktail cherry,
  to decorate

>1 Put the cracked ice cubes
into a chilled highball glass.
Pour over the tequila.

>2 Top up with orange juice.

> **>3** Stir well to mix.

> **>4** Slowly pour over the grenadine. Decorate with the orange slice and cocktail cherry.

Serve immediately.

tequila slammer

serves 1

ingredients
1 measure silver
  tequila, chilled
juice of ½ lemon
sparkling wine, chilled

>1 Put the tequila into a chilled glass.

>2 Add the lemon juice.

>3 Top up with sparkling wine.

>4 Cover the glass with your hand and slam to mix.

Serve immediately.

vodka & gin cocktails

apple martini

serves 1

ingredients
4–6 cracked ice
  cubes
1 measure vodka
1 measure sour
  apple schnapps
1 measure apple
  juice
apple wedge,
  to decorate

>1 Put the cracked ice cubes into a cocktail shaker.

>2 Pour in the vodka, schnapps and apple juice.

Serve immediately.

>3 Shake vigorously until well frosted.

>4 Strain into a chilled cocktail glass and decorate with the apple wedge.

69

metropolitan

serves 1

ingredients
1 lemon wedge
1 tbsp caster sugar
4–6 cracked ice
  cubes
½ measure vodka
½ measure
  framboise liqueur
½ measure
  cranberry juice
½ measure orange
  juice

>1 Rub the rim of a cocktail glass with the lemon wedge.

>2 Dip into the sugar, to coat.

Serve immediately.

>3 Put the cracked ice cubes into a cocktail shaker and pour over the liquid ingredients.

>4 Cover and shake, until the outside of the shaker is frosted. Strain into the glass.

71

fuzzy navel

serves 1

ingredients
4–6 cracked ice
  cubes
2 measures vodka
1 measure peach
  schnapps
225 ml/8 fl oz orange
  juice

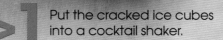 **>1** Put the cracked ice cubes into a cocktail shaker.

>2 Pour the liquid ingredients over the ice cubes.

Serve immediately.

>3 Shake vigorously until well frosted.

>4 Strain into a chilled cocktail glass.

aurora borealis

serves 1

ingredients
1 measure grappa
  or vodka, iced
1 measure green
  Chartreuse, iced
½ measure orange
  curaçao, iced
few drops crème
  de cassis, iced

>1 Pour the grappa slowly over the back of a spoon around one side of a well chilled shot glass.

>2 Gently pour the Chartreuse around the other side.

74

>3 Pour the curaçao gently into the middle.

>4 Add a few drops of crème de cassis.

Serve immediately.

peartini

serves 1

ingredients
1 tsp caster sugar
pinch ground
  cinnamon
1 lemon wedge
4–6 cracked ice
  cubes
1 measure vodka
1 measure pear
  brandy

>1 Mix the sugar and cinnamon in a saucer.

>2 Rub the rim of a cocktail glass with the lemon wedge.

Serve immediately.

>3 Dip into the sugar and cinnamon mixture, to coat.

>4 Put the cracked ice cubes into a cocktail shaker and pour in the vodka and pear brandy. Stir well and strain into the glass.

salty dog

serves 1

ingredients
1 tbsp granulated
  sugar
1 tbsp coarse salt
1 lime wedge
cracked ice cubes
2 measures vodka
grapefruit juice

>**1** Mix the sugar and salt in a saucer.

>**2** Rub the rim of a chilled cocktail glass with the lime wedge.

>3 Dip into the sugar and salt mixture, to coat.

Serve immediately.

>4 Fill the glass with cracked ice cubes and pour over the vodka. Top up with the grapefruit juice and stir.

sex on the beach

serves 1

ingredients
crushed ice
1 measure peach
   schnapps
1 measure vodka
2 measures fresh
   orange juice
3 measures cranberry
   and peach juice
dash lemon juice
orange peel twist,
   to decorate

>1 Put 4–6 crushed ice cubes into a cocktail shaker and pour over the peach schnapps, vodka, orange juice and cranberry and peach juice.

>2 Shake until well frosted.

>3 Strain into a glass filled with crushed ice.

>4 Squeeze over the lemon juice and decorate with the orange peel.

Serve immediately.

a sloe kiss

serves 1

ingredients
4–6 cracked ice
  cubes
½ measure sloe gin
½ measure
  Southern Comfort
1 measure vodka
1 tsp amaretto
splash of Galliano
orange juice
orange peel twist,
  to decorate

>1 Put the cracked ice cubes into a cocktail shaker, pour over the sloe gin, Southern Comfort, vodka and amaretto and shake until well frosted.

>2 Strain into a long, chilled glass filled with cracked ice.

>3 Splash on the Galliano.

>4 Top up with orange juice and decorate with the orange peel.

Serve immediately.

kamikaze

serves 1

ingredients
4–6 cracked ice
  cubes
1 measure vodka
1 measure Triple Sec
½ measure fresh lime
  juice
½ measure fresh
  lemon juice
dry white wine,
  chilled
cucumber and lime
  slices, to decorate

>1 Put the cracked ice cubes into a cocktail shaker.

>2 Pour over the vodka, Triple Sec, lime juice and lemon juice and shake until well frosted.

>3 Strain into a chilled glass.

>4 Top up with wine and decorate with the cucumber and lime slices.

Serve immediately.

seabreeze

serves 1

ingredients
4–6 cracked ice
  cubes
1½ measures vodka
½ measure
  cranberry juice
pink grapefruit juice

>1 Put the cracked ice cubes into a cocktail shaker.

>2 Pour over the vodka and cranberry juice and shake until frosted.

> **3** Strain into a chilled tumbler.

> **4** Top up with pink grapefruit juice.

Serve immediately.

mimi

serves 1

ingredients
2 measures vodka
½ measure
 coconut cream
2 measures
 pineapple juice
4–6 crushed ice
 cubes
fresh pineapple
 slice, to decorate

>1 Put the vodka, coconut cream, pineapple juice and crushed ice in a blender.

>2 Blend for a few seconds until frothy.

> **>3** Pour into a chilled cocktail glass.

Serve immediately.

> **>4** Decorate with a slice of pineapple.

cranberry collins

serves 1

ingredients
cracked ice cubes
2 measures vodka
¾ measure elderflower
  cordial
3 measures cranberry
  juice
soda water
lime slice and lime peel
  twist, to decorate

>1 Put 4–6 cracked ice cubes into a cocktail shaker.

>2 Pour over the vodka, elderflower cordial and cranberry juice and shake until well frosted.

>3 Strain into a Collins glass filled with cracked ice.

>4 Top up with soda water and decorate with the lime slice and peel.

Serve immediately.

flying grasshopper

serves 1

ingredients

4–6 cracked ice
  cubes
1 measure vodka
1 measure green
  crème de menthe
1 measure crème
  de cacao
fresh mint,
  to decorate

>1 Put the cracked ice cubes
into a mixing glass.

>2 Pour over the vodka, crème de
menthe and crème de cacao.

>3 Stir well.

Serve immediately.

>4 Strain into a chilled cocktail glass and decorate with a sprig of fresh mint.

vodka espresso

serves 1

ingredients

4–6 cracked ice
  cubes
2 measures
  espresso or other
  strong black
  coffee, cooled
1 measure vodka
2 tsp caster sugar
1 measure Amarula

>1 Put the cracked ice into a cocktail shaker.

>2 Pour in the coffee and vodka, add the sugar and shake vigorously until well frosted.

Serve immediately.

>**3** Strain into a chilled cocktail glass.

>**4** Float the Amarula on top.

belle collins

serves 1

ingredients
2 fresh mint sprigs,
  plus extra to
  decorate
2 measures gin
1 measure lemon
  juice
1 tsp sugar syrup
4–6 crushed ice
  cubes
sparkling water

>1 Muddle the mint sprigs.

>2 Place the mint in a chilled tumbler and pour in the gin, lemon juice and sugar syrup.

>3 Add the crushed ice cubes to the glass.

>4 Top up with sparkling water, stir gently and decorate with more fresh mint.

Serve immediately.

teardrop

serves 1

ingredients
1 measure gin
2 measures apricot
  nectar or peach
  nectar
1 measure single
  cream
crushed ice
½ measure
  strawberry syrup
fresh strawberry
  and peach slices,
  to decorate

>1 Put the gin, apricot nectar and cream into a blender.

>2 Blend for 5–10 seconds until thick and frothy.

Serve immediately.

>3 Pour into a long glass filled with crushed ice.

>4 Splash the strawberry syrup on the top and decorate with the strawberry and peach slices.

bleu bleu bleu

serves 1

ingredients
crushed ice
1 measure gin
1 measure vodka
1 measure tequila
1 measure fresh
  lemon juice
2 dashes egg white
1 measure blue
  curaçao
soda water
lemon slice,
  to decorate

>1 Put 4–6 crushed ice cubes into a cocktail shaker.

>2 Add the gin, vodka, tequila, lemon juice and egg white.

>3 Add the curaçao and shake until frosted.

>4 Strain the cocktail into a tall glass filled with crushed ice and top up with soda water. Decorate with a lemon slice.

Serve immediately.

101

gin rickey

serves 1

ingredients
cracked ice
2 measures gin
1 measure lime
 juice
soda water
lemon slice,
 to decorate

>1 Fill a chilled highball glass or goblet with cracked ice.

>2 Pour over the gin and lime juice.

Serve immediately.

>3 Top up with soda water.

>4 Stir gently to mix and decorate with a lemon slice.

103

blue blooded

serves 1

ingredients
1 measure gin
1 measure passion
 fruit nectar
4 cubes melon or
 mango
cracked ice
1–2 tsp blue
 curaçao

>1 Put the gin, passion fruit nectar, melon cubes and 4–6 cracked ice cubes into a blender.

>2 Blend until smooth and frosted.

Serve immediately.

>3 Pour into a tall, chilled glass filled with cracked ice.

>4 Top with the curaçao.

daisy

serves 1

ingredients
4–6 cracked ice
  cubes
3 measures gin
1 measure lemon
  juice
1 tbsp grenadine
1 tsp sugar syrup
soda water
orange wedge,
  to decorate

>1 Put the cracked ice cubes into a cocktail shaker.

>2 Pour over the gin, lemon juice, grenadine and sugar syrup and shake vigorously until well frosted.

>3 Strain the cocktail into a chilled highball glass.

>4 Top up with soda water, stir gently and decorate with the orange wedge.

Serve immediately.

pink pussycat

serves 1

ingredients
cracked ice
dash grenadine
2 measures gin
pineapple juice
pineapple slice,
  to decorate

>1 Half fill a chilled tumbler with cracked ice.

>2 Dash the grenadine over the ice.

>3 Pour in the gin.

>4 Top up with pineapple juice and decorate with the pineapple slice.

Serve immediately.

bloodhound

serves 1

ingredients
2 measures gin
1 measure sweet
vermouth
1 measure dry
vermouth
3 strawberries, plus
one to decorate
4–6 cracked ice
cubes

>1 Put the gin, sweet vermouth, dry vermouth and strawberries into a blender.

>2 Add the cracked ice.

>3 Blend until smooth.

Serve immediately.

>4 Pour into a chilled cocktail glass and decorate with the remaining strawberry.

dirty martini

serves 1

ingredients
4–6 cracked ice
  cubes
3 measures gin
1 measure dry
  vermouth
½ measure brine
  (from jar of
  cocktail olives)
cocktail olive,
  to decorate

>1 Put the cracked ice into a cocktail shaker.

>2 Pour over the gin, vermouth and brine.

Serve immediately.

>3 Shake vigorously until well frosted.

>4 Strain into a chilled cocktail glass and decorate with the olive.

dry martini

serves 1

ingredients
4–6 cracked ice
  cubes
1 measure London
  dry gin
dash dry vermouth
cocktail olive,
  to decorate

>1 Put the cracked ice into a cocktail shaker.

>2 Pour over the gin and vermouth.

>**3** Shake until well frosted.

>**4** Strain into a chilled glass and decorate with the olive.

Serve immediately.

115

alexander

serves 1

ingredients
 4–6 cracked ice
  cubes
1 measure gin
1 measure crème
  de cacao
1 measure single
  cream
freshly grated
  nutmeg, to
  decorate

>1 Put the cracked ice cubes into a cocktail shaker.

>2 Pour over the gin, crème de cacao and cream and shake vigorously until well frosted.

>3 Strain into a chilled cocktail glass.

>4 Sprinkle over the grated nutmeg.

Serve immediately.

whiskey & rum cocktails

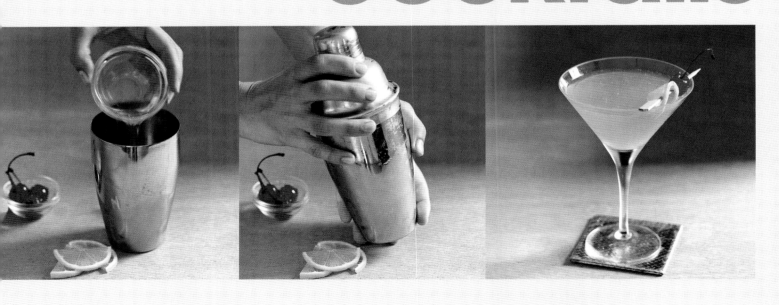

whiskey sour

serves 1

ingredients
4–6 cracked ice
   cubes
1 measure lime juice
2 measures blended
   whiskey
1 tsp icing sugar or
   sugar syrup
lime slice and
   cocktail cherry,
   to decorate

>1 Put the cracked ice cubes into a cocktail shaker.

>2 Pour over the lime juice and whiskey.

Serve immediately.

>3 Add the sugar and shake well.

>4 Strain into a cocktail glass and decorate with the slice of lime and a cherry.

mint julep

serves 1

ingredients
1 fresh mint sprig,
  plus extra to
  decorate
1 tbsp sugar syrup
cracked ice
3 measures
  bourbon

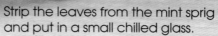 Strip the leaves from the mint sprig
and put in a small chilled glass.

 Crush the mint leaves and pour in
the sugar syrup.

>3 Half-fill the glass with cracked ice and stir.

>4 Add the bourbon and decorate with the remaining mint sprig.

Serve immediately.

french kiss

serves 1

ingredients
4–6 cracked ice
  cubes
2 measures
  bourbon
1 measure apricot
  liqueur
2 tsp grenadine
1 tsp lemon juice

>1 Put the cracked ice cubes into a cocktail shaker.

>2 Pour over the liquid ingredients.

Serve immediately.

>3 Shake vigorously until well frosted.

>4 Strain into a chilled cocktail glass.

miami beach

serves 1

ingredients
4–6 cracked ice
  cubes
2 measures Scotch
  whisky
1½ measures dry
  vermouth
2 measures pink
  grapefruit juice
orange peel strip,
  to decorate

>1 Put the cracked ice cubes into a cocktail shaker.

>2 Pour over the whisky, vermouth and grapefruit juice.

Serve immediately.

>3 Shake vigorously until well frosted. Strain into a chilled cocktail glass.

>4 Decorate with the orange peel strip.

highland fling

serves 1

ingredients
4–6 cracked ice cubes
dash of Angostura bitters
2 measures Scotch whisky
1 measure sweet vermouth
cocktail olive, to decorate

>1 Put the cracked ice into a mixing glass.

>2 Pour over the Angostura bitters.

>3 Pour in the whisky and vermouth and stir well to mix.

>4 Strain into a chilled glass and decorate with the olive.

Serve immediately.

whiskey sling

serves 1

ingredients
1 tsp icing sugar
1 measure lemon
 juice
1 tsp water
2 measures
 American
 blended whiskey
cracked ice
orange wedge,
 to decorate

>1 Put the sugar into a mixing glass.

>2 Add the lemon juice and water and stir until the sugar has dissolved.

>3 Pour in the whiskey and stir to mix.

>4 Half-fill a small chilled tumbler with cracked ice and strain the cocktail over it. Decorate with the orange wedge.

Serve immediately.

queen of memphis

serves 1

ingredients

4–6 cracked ice
  cubes
2 measures
  bourbon
1 measure Midori
1 measure peach
  juice
dash of maraschino
  liqueur
melon wedge,
  to decorate

>1 Put the cracked ice cubes into a cocktail shaker.

>2 Pour over the bourbon, Midori, peach juice and maraschino. Shake vigorously until well frosted.

Serve immediately.

>3 Strain into a chilled cocktail glass.

>4 Decorate with the melon wedge.

whiskey rickey

serves 1

ingredients

4–6 crushed ice
 cubes
2 measures whiskey
1 measure lime
 juice
soda water
lime slice, to
 decorate

 **>1** Put the crushed ice into a chilled highball glass.

>2 Pour over the whiskey and lime juice.

134

>3 Top up with soda water.

>4 Stir gently to mix and decorate with the lime slice.

Serve immediately.

135

klondike cooler

serves 1

ingredients
½ tsp icing sugar
1 measure ginger
  ale
cracked ice
2 measures
  blended whiskey
sparkling water
lemon peel twist,
  to decorate

>1 Put the sugar into a chilled tumbler and add the ginger ale. Stir until the sugar has dissolved.

>2 Fill the glass with cracked ice.

>**3** Pour over the whiskey.

>**4** Top up with sparkling water. Stir gently and decorate with the lemon peel.

Serve immediately.

boston sour

serves 1

ingredients
4–6 cracked ice
  cubes
1 measure lemon
  juice or lime juice
2 measures
  blended whiskey
1 tsp sugar syrup
1 egg white
lemon slice and
  cocktail cherry,
  to decorate

>1 Put the cracked ice cubes
into a cocktail shaker.

>2 Pour over the lemon juice, whiskey
and sugar syrup.

Serve immediately.

>3 Add the egg white.

>4 Shake until chilled. Strain into a cocktail glass and decorate with the lemon slice and a cocktail cherry.

139

whiskey sangaree

serves 1

ingredients
4–6 ice cubes
2 measures
   bourbon
1 tsp sugar syrup
soda water
1 tbsp ruby port
freshly grated
   nutmeg, to
   decorate

>1 Put the ice in a chilled tumbler.

>2 Pour over the bourbon and sugar syrup.

>3 Top up with soda water.

>4 Stir gently to mix, then float the port on top. Sprinkle over some of the grated nutmeg.

Serve immediately.

shamrock

serves 1

ingredients
4–6 cracked ice cubes
1 measure Irish whiskey
1 measure dry vermouth
3 dashes of green Chartreuse
3 dashes of crème de menthe

>1 Put the cracked ice into a mixing glass.

>2 Pour over the whiskey, vermouth and Chartreuse.

Serve immediately.

>3 Stir until well frosted.

>4 Strain into a chilled cocktail glass, pour over the crème de menthe and stir.

143

bourbon milk punch

serves 1

ingredients

4–6 cracked ice
  cubes
2 measures
  bourbon
3 measures milk
dash of vanilla
  extract
1 tsp clear honey
freshly grated
  nutmeg, to
  decorate

>1 Put the cracked ice cubes into a cocktail shaker.

>2 Pour over the bourbon, milk and vanilla extract.

>3 Add the honey and shake until well frosted.

>4 Strain into a chilled tumbler. Sprinkle over the grated nutmeg.

Serve immediately.

cuba libre

serves 1

ingredients
cracked ice
2 measures
  white rum
cola
lime wedge,
  to decorate

>1 Half-fill a highball glass with cracked ice.

>2 Pour over the rum.

Serve immediately.

>3 Top up with cola.

>4 Stir gently to mix and decorate with the lime wedge.

mellow mule

serves 1

ingredients
4–6 cracked ice
  cubes
2 measures white
  rum
1 measure dark rum
1 measure golden
  rum
1 measure falernum
  (wine-based ginger
  syrup)
1 measure lime juice
ginger beer
pineapple wedges
  and stem ginger,
  to decorate

>1 Put the cracked ice cubes into a cocktail shaker.

>2 Pour over the white rum, dark rum, golden rum, falernum and lime juice and shake vigorously until well frosted.

>3 Strain the cocktail into a tall, chilled tumbler.

>4 Top up with ginger beer and decorate with the pineapple wedges and ginger.

Serve immediately.

bajan sun

serves 1

ingredients
4–6 crushed ice
  cubes
1 measure white
  rum
1 measure
  mandarin brandy
1 measure fresh
  orange juice
1 measure
  pineapple juice
splash of grenadine
fresh pineapple
  slice and a
  cocktail cherry,
  to decorate

>1 Put the crushed ice into a cocktail shaker.

>2 Pour over the rum, brandy, orange juice and pineapple juice.

150

>3 Add the grenadine and shake vigorously.

>4 Strain into a tall, chilled glass and decorate with the pineapple slice and cocktail cherry.

Serve immediately.

frozen peach daiquiri

serves 1

ingredients
4–6 crushed ice
  cubes
½ peach, stoned
  and chopped
2 measures white
  rum
1 measure lime
  juice
1 tsp sugar syrup
peach slice,
  to decorate

>1 Put the crushed ice and the peach into a blender.

>2 Add the rum, lime juice and sugar syrup and blend until slushy.

>3 Pour into a chilled cocktail glass.

Serve immediately.

>4 Decorate with the peach slice.

cuban special

serves 1

ingredients
4–6 cracked ice
  cubes
2 measures white
  rum
1 measure lime
  juice
1 tbsp pineapple
  juice
1 tsp Triple Sec
pineapple wedges,
  to decorate

>1 Put the cracked ice cubes into a cocktail shaker.

>2 Pour over the rum, lime juice, pineapple juice and Triple Sec.

154

Serve immediately.

>3 Shake vigorously until well frosted. Strain into a chilled cocktail glass.

>4 Decorate with the pineapple wedges.

ocean breeze

serves 1

ingredients
4–6 crushed ice
  cubes
1 measure white
  rum
1 measure
  amaretto
½ measure blue
  curaçao
½ measure
  pineapple juice
soda water

> **1** Put the crushed ice into a cocktail shaker.

> **2** Pour over the white rum, amaretto, blue curaçao and pineapple juice and shake well.

>3 Strain into a tall, chilled glass.

>4 Top up with soda water.

Serve immediately.

strawberry colada

serves 1

ingredients

4–6 crushed ice
  cubes
3 measures golden
  rum
4 measures
  pineapple juice
1 measure coconut
  cream
6 strawberries
pineapple wedge,
  and halved
  strawberry, to
  decorate

>1 Put the crushed ice in a blender.

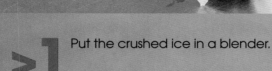

>2 Add the rum, pineapple juice and coconut cream.

>3 Hull the strawberries and add to the blender. Blend until smooth.

>4 Pour, without straining, into a tall, chilled tumbler. Decorate with the pineapple wedge and strawberry.

Serve immediately.

plantation punch

serves 1

ingredients
4–6 cracked ice
  cubes
2 measures dark
  rum
1 measure
  Southern Comfort
1 measure lemon
  juice
1 tsp brown sugar
sparkling water
1 tsp ruby port

>1 Put the cracked ice cubes into a cocktail shaker. Add the rum, Southern Comfort, lemon juice and brown sugar.

>2 Shake vigorously until well frosted. Strain into a tall, chilled glass.

> **>3** Top up with sparkling water.

> **>4** Float the port on top by pouring it gently over the back of a teaspoon.

Serve immediately.

blue hawaiian

serves 1

ingredients
4–6 crushed ice
 cubes
2 measures Bacardi
 rum
½ measure blue
 curaçao
1 measure
 pineapple juice
½ measure
 coconut cream
pineapple wedge,
 to decorate

>1 Put the crushed ice in a cocktail shaker.

>2 Pour over the liquid ingredients.

>3 Shake vigorously until well frosted. Strain into a chilled wine goblet.

>4 Decorate with the pineapple wedge.

Serve immediately.

josiah's bay float

serves 1

ingredients

4–6 cracked ice cubes
2 measures golden rum
1 measure Galliano
2 measures pineapple juice
1 measure lime juice
4 tsp sugar syrup
scooped-out pineapple shell, to serve
champagne
lime slices, lemon slices and cocktail cherries, to decorate

>1 Put the cracked ice cubes into a cocktail shaker.

>2 Pour over the rum, Galliano, pineapple juice, lime juice and sugar syrup and shake vigorously until well frosted.

>3 Strain into the pineapple shell.

>4 Top up with champagne and decorate with the lime and lemon slices and cocktail cherries.

Serve immediately.

banana daiquiri

serves 1

ingredients
2 measures white
 rum, chilled
½ measure Triple
 Sec, chilled
½ measure lime
 juice
½ measure single
 cream, chilled
1 tsp sugar syrup
¼ banana, peeled
 and sliced
lime slice,
 to decorate

>1 Put all the liquid ingredients into a blender.

>2 Add the banana and blend until smooth.

>3 Pour, without straining, into a chilled tumbler.

>4 Decorate with the lime slice.

Serve immediately.

rum cooler

serves 1

ingredients
cracked ice
1½ measures white
 rum
1½ measures
 pineapple juice
1 banana, peeled
 and sliced
juice of 1 lime
lime peel twist,
 to decorate

>1 Put 2–4 cracked ice cubes, the rum, pineapple juice and banana into a blender.

>2 Add the lime juice and blend for about 1 minute or until smooth.

>**3** Fill a chilled glass with cracked ice and pour over the cocktail.

>**4** Decorate with the lime peel.

Serve immediately.

bubbles, liqueurs & virgin cocktails

champagne cocktail

serves 1

ingredients
1 sugar cube
2 dashes Angostura
 bitters
1 measure brandy
champagne, chilled

>1 Place the sugar cube in
the bottom of a chilled
champagne flute.

>2 Add the Angostura bitters.

Serve immediately.

>3 Pour over the brandy.

>4 Top up with champagne.

kir royale

serves 1

ingredients
few drops crème de
 cassis, or to taste
½ measure brandy
champagne, chilled
fresh mint spring,
 to decorate

>1 Put the cassis into the bottom of a champagne flute.

>2 Add the brandy.

>3 Top up with champagne.

>4 Decorate with the mint sprig.

Serve immediately.

175

monte carlo

serves 1

ingredients
4–6 ice cubes
½ measure gin
¼ measure lemon
  juice
champagne or
  sparkling white
  wine, chilled
¼ measure crème
  de menthe
fresh mint sprig,
  to decorate

>1 Put the ice into a mixing glass, pour over the gin and lemon juice.

>2 Stir until well chilled.

>3 Strain into a chilled champagne flute and top up with champagne.

>4 Drizzle the crème de menthe over the top and decorate with the mint sprig.

Serve immediately.

177

flirtini

serves 1

ingredients

¼ slice fresh
  pineapple,
  chopped
½ measure chilled
  Cointreau
½ measure chilled
  vodka
1 measure chilled
  pineapple juice
champagne, chilled

>1 Put the pineapple into a mixing glass or jug.

>2 Crush the pineapple and add the Cointreau, vodka and pineapple juice. Stir well.

>3 Strain into a glass.

>4 Top up with champagne.

Serve immediately.

peacemaker

serves 4

ingredients

25 strawberries, hulled
½ small fresh pineapple, peeled and crushed
1–2 tbsp icing sugar,
1 measure maraschino
225 ml/8 fl oz sparkling water
1 bottle dry champagne
fresh mint leaves and sliced strawberries, to decorate

>1 Put the fruit and sugar into a large punch bowl.

>2 Add a little water and crush together.

>**3** Add the maraschino and sparkling water and mix well.

>**4** Top up with the champagne. Decorate with the mint leaves and strawberry slices.

Serve immediately.

champagne pick-me-up

serves 1

ingredients

4–6 cracked ice
  cubes
2 measures brandy
1 measure orange
  juice
1 measure lemon
  juice
dash grenadine
champagne,
  chilled

>1 Put the cracked ice cubes into a cocktail shaker.

>2 Pour over the brandy, orange juice, lemon juice and grenadine and shake vigorously until well frosted.

Serve immediately.

>3 Strain into a chilled wine glass.

>4 Top up with champagne.

B-52

serves 1

ingredients
1 measure chilled dark crème de cacao
1 measure chilled Bailey's Irish Cream
1 measure chilled Grand Marnier

>1 Pour the crème de cacao into a shot glass.

>2 With a steady hand, gently pour in the Bailey's to make a second layer.

>3 Gently pour in the Grand Marnier.

>4 Cover with your hand and slam to mix, or alternatively serve with layers intact.

Serve immediately.

tricolour

serves 1

ingredients
1 measure chilled
 red maraschino
 liqueur
1 measure chilled
 crème de menthe
1 measure chilled
 Bailey's Irish
 Cream
fresh mint leaf,
 to decorate

>1 Pour the maraschino into a chilled shot glass.

>2 Gently pour in the crème de menthe to make a second layer.

>3 Gently pour in the Bailey's Irish Cream.

>4 Decorate with the mint leaf.

Serve immediately.

rattlesnake

serves 1

ingredients

1 measure chilled
dark crème de
cacao
1 measure chilled
Bailey's Irish
Cream
1 measure chilled
Kahlúa
cocktail cherry,
to decorate

>1 Pour the crème de cacao into a shot glass.

>2 With a steady hand, gently pour in the Bailey's Irish Cream to make a second layer.

188

>3 Pour in the Kahlúa to make a third layer. Do not stir.

>4 Decorate with the cherry.

Serve immediately.

sangria

serves 6

ingredients
juice of 1 orange
juice of 1 lemon
2 tbsp icing sugar
cracked ice
1 orange, thinly
  sliced
1 lemon, thinly
  sliced
1 bottle chilled red
  wine
lemonade,
  to taste

>1 Put the orange juice and lemon juice in a large jug. Stir.

>2 Add the sugar and stir. When the sugar has dissolved, add 4–6 cracked ice cubes.

> **>3** Add the sliced fruit and the wine and marinate for 1 hour.

> **>4** Add lemonade to taste, then top up with cracked ice.

Serve immediately.

brandy alexander

serves 1

ingredients
4–6 cracked ice
  cubes
1 measure brandy
1 measure dark
  crème de cacao
1 measure double
  cream
freshly grated
  nutmeg, to
  decorate

>**1** Put the cracked ice cubes into a cocktail shaker.

>**2** Pour over the brandy, crème de cacao and cream and shake vigorously until well frosted.

Serve immediately.

>**3** Strain into a chilled cocktail glass.

>**4** Sprinkle over the grated nutmeg.

ginger fizz

serves 1

ingredients
ginger ale
fresh mint sprigs
cracked ice
fresh raspberries
   and a sprig of
   mint, to decorate

>1 Put 2 measures of ginger ale into a blender.

>2 Add a few mint sprigs and blend together.

> **3** Strain into a chilled highball glass two-thirds filled with cracked ice and top up with more ginger ale.

> **4** Decorate with raspberries and the mint sprig.

Serve immediately.

shirley temple

serves 1

ingredients
cracked ice cubes
2 measures lemon
 juice
½ measure
 grenadine
½ measure sugar
 syrup
ginger ale
orange slice,
 to decorate

>1 Put 4–6 cracked ice cubes into a cocktail shaker.

>2 Pour over the lemon juice, grenadine and sugar syrup and shake vigorously until well frosted.

>3 Half-fill a chilled highball glass with cracked ice, then strain the cocktail over it.

>4 Top up with ginger ale and decorate with the orange slice.

Serve immediately.

mini colada

serves 1

ingredients
cracked ice cubes
6 measures milk
3 measures
  coconut cream
4 measures
  pineapple juice

to decorate
pineapple cubes
pineapple leaf
cocktail cherry

> **>1** Put 4–6 cracked ice cubes into a cocktail shaker.

> **>2** Pour over the milk and coconut cream.

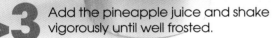

>3 Add the pineapple juice and shake vigorously until well frosted.

>4 Half-fill a highball glass with cracked ice, strain the cocktail into it and decorate with the pineapple cubes, pineapple leaf and cherry.

Serve immediately.

faux kir royale

serves 1

ingredients
4–6 cracked ice
  cubes
1½ measures
  raspberry syrup
sparkling apple
  juice, chilled

>1 Put the cracked ice cubes into a mixing glass. Pour over the raspberry syrup.

>2 Stir well to mix.

Serve immediately.

>3 Strain into a chilled wine glass.

>4 Top up with sparkling apple juice and stir.

201

maidenly
mimosa

serves 2

ingredients
175 ml/6 fl oz
  orange juice
175 ml/6 fl oz
  sparkling white
  grape juice
orange slices,
  to decorate

>1 Chill two champagne flutes.

>2 Divide the orange juice between
the flutes.

Serve immediately.

>3 Top up with the sparkling grape juice.

>4 Decorate with the orange slice.

cool collins

serves 1

ingredients
6 fresh mint leaves,
 plus extra to
 decorate
1 tsp caster sugar
2 measures lemon
 juice
cracked ice cubes
sparkling water
lemon slice,
 to decorate

>1 Put the mint leaves into a chilled Collins glass.

>2 Add the sugar and lemon juice.

> **>3** Crush the mint leaves, then stir until the sugar has dissolved.

> **>4** Fill the glass with cracked ice cubes and top up with sparkling water. Stir gently and decorate with the fresh mint and lemon slice.

Serve immediately.

prohibition punch

serves 6

ingredients
850 ml/1½ pints
  apple juice
350 ml/12 fl oz
  lemon juice
125 ml/4 fl oz sugar
  syrup
cracked ice cubes
2¼ litres/4 pints
  ginger ale
orange slices,
  to decorate

>1 Pour the apple juice into a large jug.

>2 Add the lemon juice and sugar syrup.

>3 Add a handful of cracked ice cubes.

>4 Pour in the ginger ale and stir gently to mix. Pour into chilled lowball glasses and decorate with the orange slices.

Serve immediately.

bright green cooler

serves 1

ingredients
cracked ice cubes
3 measures
  pineapple juice
2 measures lime
  juice
1 measure green
  peppermint syrup
ginger ale
cucumber strip and
  lime slice,
  to decorate

> **>1** Put 4–6 cracked ice cubes into a cocktail shaker.

> **>2** Pour over the pineapple juice, lime juice and peppermint syrup and shake vigorously until well frosted.

> **3** Half-fill a chilled highball glass with cracked ice and strain the cocktail over it.

> **4** Top up with ginger ale and decorate with the cucumber strip and lime slice.

209

virgin mary

serves 1

ingredients

4–6 cracked ice
  cubes
3 measures tomato
  juice
1 measure lemon
  juice
2 dashes
  Worcestershire
  sauce
1 dash hot pepper
  sauce
pinch celery salt
pepper
lemon wedge and
  celery stick,
  to decorate

>1 Put the cracked ice cubes into a cocktail shaker. Pour over the tomato juice.

>2 Add the lemon juice.

Serve immediately.

>**3** Pour in the Worcestershire sauce and hot pepper sauce. Shake vigorously until well frosted.

>**4** Season with the celery salt and pepper, strain into a chilled glass and decorate with the lemon wedge and celery stick.

mango lassi

serves 2

ingredients

225 ml/8 fl oz milk
125 ml/4 fl oz
  natural yogurt
1 tbsp rosewater
3 tbsp honey
1 ripe mango,
  peeled and diced
4–6 ice cubes
rose petals,
  to decorate
  (optional)

>1 Pour the milk and yogurt into a blender and process until combined.

>2 Add the rosewater and honey and process until blended.

>3 Add the mango and ice cubes and blend until smooth.

>4 Pour into two chilled glasses and decorate with the rose petals, if using.

Serve immediately.

raspberry lemonade

serves 4

ingredients
2 lemons
115 g/4 oz icing
   sugar
115 g/4 oz
   raspberries
few drops vanilla
   extract
cracked ice cubes
sparkling water
fresh mint sprigs,
   to decorate

> **1** Cut the ends off the lemons, then scoop out and chop the flesh.

> **2** Put the lemon flesh in a blender with the sugar, raspberries, vanilla extract and 4–6 cracked ice cubes and blend for 2–3 minutes.

>3 Half-fill four highball glasses with cracked ice and strain in the lemonade.

>4 Top up with sparkling water and decorate with the mint sprigs.

Serve immediately.

coconut cream

serves 2

ingredients
350 ml/12 fl oz
  pineapple juice
90ml/3¼ fl oz
  coconut milk
150 g/5½ oz vanilla
  ice cream
140 g/5 oz frozen
  pineapple chunks
grated fresh
  coconut, to
  decorate

>1 Pour the pineapple juice and coconut milk into a blender.

>2 Add the ice cream and process until smooth.

>3 Add the pineapple chunks and process until smooth.

>4 Divide between two chilled glasses and decorate with the grated coconut.

Serve immediately.

heavenly days

serves 1

ingredients
cracked ice
2 measures
  hazelnut syrup
2 measures lemon
  juice
1 tsp grenadine
sparkling water

>1 Put 4–6 cracked ice cubes into a cocktail shaker.

>2 Pour over the hazelnut syrup, lemon juice and grenadine and shake vigorously until well frosted.

>**3** Half-fill a tumbler with cracked ice and strain the cocktail over.

>**4** Top up with sparkling water and stir gently.

Serve immediately.

apple pie
cream

serves 1

ingredients
4–6 cracked ice
  cubes
4 measures apple
  juice
1 small scoop
  vanilla ice cream
soda water
cinnamon sugar
  and apple slice,
  to decorate

>1 Put the cracked ice cubes into a blender and add the apple juice and ice cream.

>2 Blend for 10–15 seconds until frothy and frosted. Pour into a chilled glass.

>3 Top up with soda water.

>4 Sprinkle over the cinnamon sugar and decorate with an apple slice.

Serve immediately.

Index